Take Care of Yourself

Getting Exercise

Siân Smith

Heinemann
L I B R A R Y

Chicago, Illinois

www.capstonepub.com
Visit our website to find out
more information about
Heinemann-Raintree books.

To order:
☎ Phone 800-747-4992
🖳 Visit www.capstonepub.com
   to browse our catalog and order online.

Edited by Dan Nunn, Rebecca Rissman,
   and John-Paul Wilkins
Designed by Victoria Allen
Picture research by Tracy Cummins
Production by Alison Parsons
Originated by Capstone Global Library Ltd
Printed and bound in China by Leo Paper Products Ltd

16 15 14 13 12
10 9 8 7 6 5 4 3 2 1

Library of Congress Cataloging-in-Publication Data
Smith, Siân.
   Getting exercise / Siân Smith.
      p. cm.—(Take care of yourself!)
   Includes bibliographical references and index.
   ISBN 978-1-4329-6710-9 (hb)—ISBN 978-1-4329-6717-8 (pb)
1. Exercise—Juvenile literature. 2. Physical fitness—Juvenile
literature. I. Title.
   RA781.S617 2013
   613.7′1—dc23   2011049839

Acknowledgments
We would like to thank the following for permission to
reproduce photographs: Capstone Publishers p. 23a; Corbis
pp. 4 © Christina Kennedy/DK Stock, 9 (© Kris Timken/
Blend Images); Getty Images pp. 8 (Photo and Co), 13
(ImagesBazaar), 19 (Jena Cumbo), 21 (Paul Debois);
istockphoto pp. 5 (© sonyae), 11, 22, 23c (© kali9), 16
(© Rhienna Cutler), 17 (© Alexander Semenov), 18 (©
Robert Dant), 20 (© Vladimir Nikitin); Shutterstock pp. 6 (©
CHRISTOPHE ROLLAND), 7 (© Morgan Lane Photography),
10 (© oliveromg), 12 (© Elena Elisseeva), 14, 23b (© Felix
Mizioznikov), 15 (© greenland).

Front cover photograph of smiling boy in a swimming pool
reproduced with permission of istockphoto (© insagostudio).
Rear cover photograph of children stretching reproduced
with permission of istockphoto (© kali9).

Every effort has been made to contact copyright holders
of material reproduced in this book. Any omissions will be
rectified in subsequent printings if notice is given to the
publisher.

We would like to thank Nancy Harris and Dee Reid for their
assistance in the preparation of this book.

Contents

Exercise

You need to get some exercise every day.

Exercise keeps your body healthy.

Every Day

Get some exercise that makes you breathe fast every day.

You could play chasing games.

Get some exercise that makes your heart beat fast every day.

You could play sports.

You could jump rope fast.

If you can, stretch before and after you exercise.

Bones

Get some exercise that makes your bones strong.

You could hop or run.

Muscles

Get some exercise that makes your muscles strong.

You could try climbing.

Gentle Exercise

Gentle exercise helps your body, too.

Walk whenever you can.

You could ride on a scooter.

You can even exercise while you play games.

Exercise makes your body strong
and helps you sleep.

Exercise can be fun!

Can You Remember?

What should you try to do before and after you exercise?

Answer on page 24

Picture Glossary

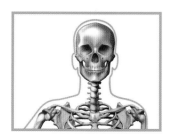 **bones** you have bones inside your body. Bones help to keep your body up.

 **muscles** stretchy parts inside your body that can make things move

 **stretch** gently pull or push parts of your body

Index

Answer to question on page 22
You should try to stretch before and after exercise.

Notes for parents and teachers
Before reading
Ask the children why exercise is important. Explain that we need to exercise to keep our bodies healthy. Exercise strengthens our bodies and keeps our hearts, muscles, and bones working well. Exercise can even help us to improve our thinking skills and sleep better.

After reading
• Divide the children into pairs and give them time to think about their three favorite ways of exercising. This can include playground games, too. Ask each pair to share their ideas, then group the children into new pairs and ask them to share their ideas again. Did this help them to find other types of exercise that they want to try? If possible, try out some of these together.

• Investigate some of the benefits of exercise with the children. Try holding an early morning exercise session every day for a week. Remind the children of the importance of warm-up and cool-down exercises during the session. Reflect upon any benefits the children feel as a result of the exercise and keep a class journal of these.